CONFESSING THE HEBREW SCRIPTURES

Adonai – Jehovah Rof•e•cha – יְהוָֹה רֹפְאֶךָ

"THE LORD YOUR HEALER"

Confessing the Hebrew Scriptures
Adonai – Jehovah Rof•e•cha: The Lord Your Healer
Copyright 2011
Jonathan Bernis

Cover and interior design by dpc&s

Published by JVMI Publishing
PO Box 31998
Phoenix, AZ 85046-1998

Printed in China
Third Printing October 2015

ISBN 978-0-9821117-2-7

CONFESSING THE HEBREW SCRIPTURES

Adonai – Jehovah Rof•e•cha – יְהֹוָה רֹפְאֶךָ

"THE LORD YOUR HEALER"

Jonathan Bernis

INTRODUCTION FROM JONATHAN BERNIS

The Power of Confession

It is my hope and prayer that this workbook will prove to be a rich blessing to your life. Over my 30+ years in ministry I have seen the fruit of confession of the Word of God. Through the process of confessing and hearing the Word, I have seen many healed, delivered and transformed. Proverbs 18:21 declares, *"death and life are in the power of the tongue."* Our confession can bring either blessings or curses upon us and those we love. It is God's desire that we use our tongues to produce blessing, life and faith according to His Word. So how do we accomplish this? How do we incorporate this biblical truth to work in our lives? The biblical principle is so very simple:

> *"So then faith cometh by hearing, and hearing by the word of God."* —Romans 10:17 KJV

From this verse, we understand that faith is built in us as we hear the Word of God. Notice, though, that hearing is mentioned twice. I believe this is because there are two kinds of hearing: hearing with our natural ears and hearing with the ears of our spirit. This is the process by which faith is deposited and released in our lives. We hear the Word of God as it is read and confessed, and over time, as we hear God's promises over and over again, it eventually drops down into our spirit, where our faith is then activated. When this incredible process happens, the promises of God become a reality in our life. This simple truth is what brings us into the reality of the salvation experience:

> **"For with the heart man believeth unto righteousness; and with the mouth confession is made unto salvation."** —Romans 10:10 KJV

This is what **biblical** confession is all about. It's about getting HIS Word… (which incidentally is His will) into our hearts, into our spirits. That's where faith must dwell in order to be activated—not the mind. Not only do we experience God's provision of salvation in this manner, but also all of the other promises given to us in Scripture are based on the same principle of "believing with the heart and confessing unto." The blessings God has provided for us in His Word, such as healing and health, deliverance, divine provision, and supernatural peace and comfort are all realized in exactly the same way. Every promise and blessing of God is acquired through faith. *But without faith, it is impossible to please Him* (Hebrews 11:6).

When God called Joshua to lead the Children of Israel into the

Promised Land after the death of Moses, He gave him the following instructions:

Only be strong and very courageous, that you may observe to do according to all the law which Moses My servant commanded you; do not turn from it to the right hand or to the left, that you may prosper wherever you go. This Book of the Law shall not depart from your mouth, but you shall meditate in it day and night, that you may observe to do according to all that is written in it. For then you will make your way prosperous, and then you will have good success.
—Joshua 1:7

That word translated "meditate" in this text is the Hebrew verb הגה *(hagah)* and literally means, "to groan, sigh, mutter, or speak." While the Christian concept of meditation is derived from the Latin word "to consider or contemplate" and has more to do with reflection—the process of deliberately focusing on specific Scriptures and reflecting on their meaning—the Hebrew has two concepts or a "dual concept" of meditation. The first, שיחה, *(seecha)* has to do with rehearing in one's mind or thoughts and is similar to the Christian concept of meditation. The other, הגה *(hagah)* is not reflection with the *mind*, but with the *mouth*—to rehearse the Word of God in speech, "to speak, talk, utter, or mutter." It is this concept and practice of meditation that the Lord tells Joshua will make him both *"prosperous and successful."*

It stands to reason that if God told Joshua that confession of His Word would make him prosperous and successful, then we also can experience the same prosperity and success he experienced if we follow the same principles.

The Significance of Hebrew

While most of us understand that the Old Testament Scriptures were written primarily in the Hebrew language, very few of us can actually read or understand Hebrew. Therefore, we are forced to read the various English translations of the Bible. And while there are many excellent translations out there, they often miss the nuances, insight, and deeper revelation found in the original Hebrew.

For example, God reveals Himself through different Hebrew names in the Tanakh (Old Testament). Names such as El Shaddai, Adonai-Yireh, Adonai-Tzidkaynu, Adonai-Nissi, Adonai-Shalom (all to be dealt with in depth in follow-up workbooks) reveal His character, His attributes, His very nature. When we dig into these names in the Hebrew, we gain extraordinary insight into who the LORD is and what He has provided for us. The benefits promised to us in the Bible, promises of healing and health, salvation, deliverance, divine provision, supernatural peace, and so on are all originally in Hebrew.

So, while there is no doubt that because the LORD is omniscient, He responds to any language and that confession of the Word of God in any language is going to release power and blessing. If we want to experience the greatest impact, the greatest depth, and the fullest meaning, we must go back to the roots. And those roots are Hebrew. The ancient Hebrew sages taught that although it was permissible to pray in other languages, praying in *Lashon HaKodesh*, the Holy Tongue, was always preferable, even if the person did not understand the words.

How to Use the Workbook and CD

You may be saying to yourself at this point, "This is all well and good, but how can I do this?" How is this possible—to confess the Scriptures in the original Hebrew without going to Bible school or seminary, without undertaking an extensive study of Hebrew? The good news is there is a way. The answer is found in a system developed by the Reform Movement of American Judaism.

As Jews immigrated to America in the late 19th and early part of the 20th century from the "*Old Country*" of Eastern and Central Europe to forge a new life free from the bitter anti-Semitism they had endured for so long, they quickly began to assimilate into American culture. Hebrew education, which was a mandatory part of their former prayer life (as well as Yiddish as a spoken language) began to disappear. In order to preserve Hebrew prayer in their synagogues, a method called *transliteration* was employed. This simple process, which we see utilized in dictionaries, uses English letters to sound out the Hebrew words. In other words, the Hebrew text is converted to English in order to read and pronounce the original Hebrew.

Let's look at a few examples to understand how this works:

- The Hebrew word for "peace" is שָׁלוֹם , *Shalom*. While you may recognize this Hebrew word from seeing it often enough, most cannot read the actual Hebrew characters. But when we use the transliteration method, it now becomes very readable: **sha•lome**

- Let's try another one. The Hebrew word for *Jerusalem is* יְרוּשָׁלַיִם . While few can read the actual Hebrew, when we apply the transliteration method, it becomes easy: **Ye•roo•sha•la•yim**

- One last example is a bit more challenging. Many Jewish prayers begin this way: *"Blessed are you, O Lord our God, King of the Universe"* in Hebrew:

בָּרוּךְ אַתָּה יְיָ אֱלֹהֵינוּ מֶלֶךְ הָעוֹלָם

Even more complex sentences such as these become easy to recite with the transliteration method and a bit of practice:

Ba•ruch a•tah Ado•nai Elo•hei•nu Me•lech Ha•o•lam

And off you go. It's that easy. No seminary training, no intensive Hebrew study. Just begin to work through the pages using this simple yet effective transliteration method and you will be confessing the Scriptures in the ancient Hebrew tongue! Each page has a Scripture promise relating to Adonai (the word used by the Jewish community in substitution for the Hebrew name translated LORD, the Tetragrammaton, often pronounced *Jehovah* or *Yaweh*) Rofecha: *The Lord Your Healer* and contains the text in Hebrew, English and English Transliteration directly from the Hebrew.

We have painstakingly worked to make sure the Hebrew text is completely accurate, which is why we use *Rofecha* rather than the traditional *Rafa* or *Rafay*. This is because the Scripture that reveals this wonderful revelation: *"For I am the LORD who heals you"* (Exodus 15:26), uses *Rofecha*.

Along with the workbook, we've included a companion CD so you can hear how each Scripture sounds when spoken by a native Israeli Hebrew speaker. I suggest you begin by playing the CD and following along in the English and transliterated Hebrew from Scripture to Scripture. After, try confessing the Hebrew transliteration along with the CD to learn which syllables to accent. In no time, you will be confessing these Scriptures in Hebrew just like a native-born Israeli. It really is that easy!

Finally, let me share with you four things to keep in mind as you put these Hebrew prayers to work for your healing and health:

1. **<u>Let the Scriptures fill your heart.</u>** As you pray and confess these powerful promises of God, ask Him to make the Word come alive in your life. Watch as your faith grows on a daily basis!

2. **<u>Be confident in the goodness of God.</u>** Since these prayers are taken directly from the Hebrew Scriptures, you can know that you are praying perfectly in line with God's will for your life.

3. **<u>Confession is a simple act of trust and obedience.</u>** This is not some mysterious, mystical act. It is simply believing and acting on the truth of God's Word. As you are diligent to exercise this powerful principle in your life day by day, you will be amazed as you watch it take hold in your life and result in transformation.

4. **<u>Know that God's promises are true.</u>** I encourage you to confess these promises of healing and health boldly and with expectation that you and your loved ones will experience exactly what God promises He will do. Remember, God is the same yesterday, today and forever.

You may wish to read through the entire book at one sitting. You may choose to take one prayer in order each day during your personal time with God. You may find specific Scriptures are particularly meaningful in your specific situation and want to listen to them again and again. No matter how you utilize this workbook, I have no doubt that if you exercise this powerful principle of confessing God's Word in your daily devotions, it **will** bear fruit. You **will** be changed…

"So shall My word be that goes forth from My mouth; It shall not return to Me void, But it shall accomplish what I please, And it shall prosper in the thing for which I sent it." —Isaiah 55:11

Rabbi Jonathan Bernis, Phoenix, Arizona

Ancient Israel wall

*A*nd [He] said, "If you diligently heed the voice of the LORD your God and do what is right in His sight, give ear to His commandments and keep all His statutes, I will put none of the diseases on you which I have brought on the Egyptians. **For I am the LORD who heals you.**"

Exodus 15:26

וַיֹּאמֶר אִם-שָׁמוֹעַ תִּשְׁמַע לְקוֹל יְהֹוָה אֱלֹהֶיךָ וְהַיָּשָׁר בְּעֵינָיו
תַּעֲשֶׂה וְהַאֲזַנְתָּ לְמִצְוֹתָיו וְשָׁמַרְתָּ כָּל-חֻקָּיו כָּל-הַמַּחֲלָה
אֲשֶׁר-שַׂמְתִּי בְמִצְרַיִם לֹא-אָשִׂים עָלֶיךָ כִּי אֲנִי יְהֹוָה רֹפְאֶךָ:

26. Va•yo•mer eem - sha•moa tish•ma le•kol Adonai Elohe•cha
ve•ha•ya•shar be•ei•nav ta•a•se ve•ha•a•zan•ta le•mitz•vo•tav
ve•sha•mar•ta kol - choo•kav kol - ha•ma•cha•la asher - sam•ti
ve•Mitz•ra•yim lo - asim ale•cha ki Ani Adonai rof•e•cha.

Jaffa, Israel, is one of the most ancient port cities in the world.

N*ow see that I, even I, am He, And there is no God besides Me; I kill and I make alive; I wound and **I heal**; Nor is there any who can deliver from My hand.*

Deuteronomy 32:39

רְאוּ עַתָּה כִּי אֲנִי אֲנִי הוּא וְאֵין אֱלֹהִים עִמָּדִי אֲנִי
אָמִית וַאֲחַיֶּה מָחַצְתִּי וַאֲנִי אֶרְפָּא וְאֵין מִיָּדִי מַצִּיל:

39. Re•oo ata ki ani ani hoo ve•eyn elo•him ee•ma•di ani amit va•a•cha•ye ma•chatz•ti va•ani er•pa ve•eyn mi•ya•di ma•tzil.

View of the Dead Sea from the ancient city of Masada

CONFESSING THE HEBREW SCRIPTURES

Adonai – Jehovah Rof•e•cha – יְהוָה רֹפְאֶךָ

"THE LORD YOUR HEALER"

"*Return and tell Hezekiah the leader of My people, 'Thus says the LORD, the God of David your father: "I have heard your prayer, I have seen your tears; surely I will **heal** you. On the third day you shall go up to the house of the LORD."*

2 Kings 20:5

שׁוּב וְאָמַרְתָּ אֶל-חִזְקִיָּהוּ נְגִיד-עַמִּי כֹּה-אָמַר יְהוָה אֱלֹהֵי
דָוִד אָבִיךָ שָׁמַעְתִּי אֶת-תְּפִלָּתֶךָ רָאִיתִי אֶת-דִּמְעָתֶךָ הִנְנִי
רֹפֵא לָךְ בַּיּוֹם הַשְּׁלִישִׁי תַּעֲלֶה בֵּית יְהוָה:

5. Shoov ve•amar•ta el - Chiz•ki•yahoo n`gid - ami ko - amar Adonai Elo•hey David avi•cha sha•ma•ati et - te•fi•la•te•cha ra•ee•ti et - dim•a•te•cha hi•ne•ni ro•fe lach ba•yom hash•li•shi ta•a•le beit Adonai.

View at the Temple Mount, Western Wall, Jerusalem, Israel

CONFESSING THE HEBREW SCRIPTURES

Adonai – Jehovah Rof•e•cha – יְהֹוָה רֹפְאֶךָ
"THE LORD YOUR HEALER"

"*If My people who are called by My name will humble themselves, and pray and seek My face, and turn from their wicked ways, then I will hear from heaven, and will forgive their sin and* **heal** *their land.*"

2 Chronicles 7:14

וְיִכָּנְעוּ עַמִּי אֲשֶׁר נִקְרָא-שְׁמִי עֲלֵיהֶם וְיִתְפַּלְלוּ וִיבַקְשׁוּ פָנַי
וְיָשֻׁבוּ מִדַּרְכֵיהֶם הָרָעִים וַאֲנִי אֶשְׁמַע מִן-הַשָּׁמַיִם וְאֶסְלַח
לְחַטָּאתָם וְאֶרְפָּא אֶת-אַרְצָם:

14. Ve•yi•kan•oo ami asher nik•ra - sh`mi a•lei•hem ve•yit•pale•loo viy•vak•shoo fa•nai ve•ya•shoo•voo mi•dar•chei•hem ha•ra•eem va•ani esh•ma min - ha•sha•ma•yim ve•es•lach le•cha•ta•tam ve•er•pa et - ar•tzam.

Wailing Wall, Jerusalem, Israel

CONFESSING THE HEBREW SCRIPTURES

Adonai – Jehovah Rof•e•cha – יְהֹוָה רֹפְאֶךָ
"THE LORD YOUR HEALER"

*A*nd the Lord listened to Hezekiah and **healed** the people.

2 Chronicles 30:20

וַיִּשְׁמַע יְהוָה אֶל-יְחִזְקִיָּהוּ וַיִּרְפָּא אֶת-הָעָם:

20. Va•yish•ma Adonai el - Ye•chiz•ki•yahoo va•yir•pa et - ha•am.

Church of All Nations (Basilica of the Agony) in Jerusalem, Israel

*H*ave mercy on me, *O LORD, for I am weak; O LORD,*
***heal** me, for my bones are troubled.*

Psalm 6:2

חָנֵּנִי יְהוָה כִּי אֻמְלַל אָנִי רְפָאֵנִי יְהוָה כִּי נִבְהֲלוּ עֲצָמָי׃

3. Cho•ne•ni Adonai ki oom•lal ani refa•eni Adonai ki niv•ha•loo atza•mai.

NOTE: In the Hebrew Bible, it is 6:3.

Cardo Street in the Old City of Jerusalem, Israel

Adonai – Jehovah Rof•e•cha – יְהוָֹה רֹפְאֶךָ
"THE LORD YOUR HEALER"

*O LORD my God, I cried out to You, And You **healed** me.*

Psalm 30:2

יְהוָֹה אֱלֹהָי שִׁוַּעְתִּי אֵלֶיךָ וַתִּרְפָּאֵנִי:

3. Adonai Elo•hai shi•va•ati e•le•cha va•tir•pa•eni.

NOTE: In the Hebrew Bible, it is 30:3.

Boat on the Sea of Galilee, Israel

I said, "LORD, be merciful to me; **Heal** my soul, for I have sinned against you."

Psalm 41:4

אֲנִי־אָמַרְתִּי יְהוָה חָנֵּנִי רְפָאָה נַפְשִׁי כִּי־חָטָאתִי לָךְ:

5. Ani - amar•ti Adonai cho•ne•ni re•fa•ah naf•shi ki - cha•ta•ti lach.

NOTE: In the Hebrew Bible, it is 41:5.

At the Wailing Wall, Jerusalem, Israel

CONFESSING THE HEBREW SCRIPTURES

Adonai – Jehovah Rof•e•cha – יְהֹוָה רֹפְאֶךָ
"THE LORD YOUR HEALER"

Why are you cast down, O my soul? And why are you disquieted within me? Hope in God; For I shall yet praise Him, the help of my countenance and my God.

Psalm 42:11

מַה-תִּשְׁתּוֹחֲחִי נַפְשִׁי וּמַה-תֶּהֱמִי עָלָי הוֹחִילִי לֵאלֹהִים
כִּי-עוֹד אוֹדֶנּוּ יְשׁוּעֹת פָּנַי וֵאלֹהָי:

11. Ma - tish•to•cha•chi naf•shi oo•ma - te•he•mi a•lai ho•chi•li le'Elohim ki - od o•de•noo ye•shoo•ot pa•nai ve•Elo•hai.

Salt in the Dead Sea, Israel

CONFESSING THE HEBREW SCRIPTURES

Adonai – Jehovah Rof•e•cha – יְהֹוָה רֹפְאֶךָ
"THE LORD YOUR HEALER"

*Bless the LORD, O my soul; And all that is within me, bless His holy name! Bless the LORD, O my soul, And forget not all His benefits: Who forgives all your iniquities, Who **heals** all your diseases...*

Psalm 103:1-3

א. לְדָוִד בָּרְכִי נַפְשִׁי אֶת-יְהוָה וְכָל-קְרָבַי אֶת-שֵׁם קָדְשׁוֹ:

ב. בָּרְכִי נַפְשִׁי אֶת-יְהוָה וְאַל-תִּשְׁכְּחִי כָּל-גְּמוּלָיו:

ג. הַסֹּלֵחַ לְכָל-עֲוֹנֵכִי הָרֹפֵא לְכָל-תַּחֲלוּאָיְכִי:

1. Le•David bar•chi naf•shi et - Adonai ve•chol - ke•ra•vai et - shem kod•sho.
2. Bar•chi naf•shi et - Adonai ve•al - tish•ke•chi kol - ge•moo•lav.
3. Ha•so•le•ach le•chol - a•vo•ne•chi ha•ro•fe le•chol - ta•cha•loo•ay•chi.

Roman aqueduct at the coast of the Mediterranean Sea in Israel

He sent His word and **healed** them, And delivered them from their destructions.

Psalm 107:20

יִשְׁלַח דְּבָרוֹ וְיִרְפָּאֵם וִימַלֵּט מִשְּׁחִיתוֹתָם:

20. Yish•lach de•va•ro ve•yir•pa•em viy•ma•let mish•chi•to•tam.

One of the thousands of ancient streets in Israel

CONFESSING THE HEBREW SCRIPTURES

Adonai – Jehovah Rof•e•cha – יְהֹוָה רֹפְאֶךָ

"THE LORD YOUR HEALER"

He heals the brokenhearted And binds up their wounds.

Psalm 147:3

הָרֹפֵא לִשְׁבוּרֵי לֵב וּמְחַבֵּשׁ לְעַצְּבוֹתָם:

3. Ha•ro•fe lish•voo•rei lev oo•me•cha•besh le•atz•vo•tam.

The wall of Temple Mount, Jerusalem, Israel

CONFESSING THE HEBREW SCRIPTURES

Adonai – Jehovah Rof•e•cha – יְהוָה רֹפְאֶךָ
"THE LORD YOUR HEALER"

*T*rust in the LORD with all thine heart; and lean not unto thine own understanding. In all thy ways acknowledge him, and he shall direct thy paths. Be not wise in thine own eyes: fear the LORD, and depart from evil. It shall be **health** to thy navel, and marrow to thy bones.

Proverbs 3:5-8 KJV

ה. בְּטַח אֶל-יְהוָה בְּכָל-לִבֶּךָ וְאֶל-בִּינָתְךָ אַל-תִּשָּׁעֵן:

ו. בְּכָל-דְּרָכֶיךָ דָעֵהוּ וְהוּא יְיַשֵּׁר אֹרְחֹתֶיךָ:

ז. אַל-תְּהִי חָכָם בְּעֵינֶיךָ יְרָא אֶת-יְהוָה וְסוּר מֵרָע:

ח. רִפְאוּת תְּהִי לְשָׁרֶּךָ וְשִׁקּוּי לְעַצְמוֹתֶיךָ:

5. Be•tach el - Adonai be•chol - li•be•cha ve•el - bi•nat•cha al - ti•sha•en.
6. Be•chol - de•ra•che•cha da•e•hoo ve•hoo ye•ya•sher or•cho•te•cha.
7. Al - te•hi cha•cham be•ei•ne•cha ye•ra et - Adonai ve•soor me•ra.
8. Rif•oot te•hi le•sha•re•cha ve•shi•kooy le•atz•mo•te•cha.

One of many such staircases in the ancient port of Jaffa

CONFESSING THE HEBREW SCRIPTURES

Adonai – Jehovah Rof•e•cha – יְהֹוָה רֹפְאֶךָ

"THE LORD YOUR HEALER"

*My son, attend to my words; incline thine ear unto my sayings. Let them not depart from thine eyes; keep them in the midst of thine heart. For they are life unto those that find them, and **health** to all their flesh.*

Proverbs 4:20-22 KJV

כ. בְּנִי לִדְבָרַי הַקְשִׁיבָה לַאֲמָרַי הַט אָזְנֶךָ:

כא. אַל-יַלִּיזוּ מֵעֵינֶיךָ שָׁמְרֵם בְּתוֹךְ לְבָבֶךָ:

כב. כִּי-חַיִּים הֵם לְמֹצְאֵיהֶם וּלְכָל-בְּשָׂרוֹ מַרְפֵּא:

20. Be•ni lid•va•rai hak•shi•va la•ama•rai hat oz•ne•cha.
21. Al - ya•li•zoo me•ei•ne•cha shom•rem be•toch le•va•ve•cha.
22. Ki - cha•yim hem le•motz•ey•hem oo•le•chol - be•sa•ro mar•pe.

A view of Jerusalem, Israel

*There is that speaketh like the piercings of a sword: but the tongue of the wise is **health**.*

Proverbs 12:18 KJV

יֵשׁ בּוֹטֶה כְּמַדְקְרוֹת חָרֶב וּלְשׁוֹן חֲכָמִים מַרְפֵּא:

18. Yesh bo•te ke•mad•ke•rot cha•rev oo•le•shon cha•cha•mim mar•pe.

Banias, a nature reserve in the Golan Heights, Israel

A wicked messenger falleth into mischief: but a faithful ambassador is **health**.

Proverbs 13:17 KJV

מַלְאָךְ רָשָׁע יִפֹּל בְּרָע וְצִיר אֱמוּנִים מַרְפֵּא:

17. Mal•ach ra•sha yi•pol be•ra ve•tzir e•moo•nim mar•pe.

Sunset in Jaffa, Israel

*P*leasant words are as an honeycomb, sweet to the soul, and **health** to the bones.

Proverbs 16:24 KJV

צוּף-דְּבַשׁ אִמְרֵי-נֹעַם מָתוֹק לַנֶּפֶשׁ וּמַרְפֵּא לָעָצֶם:

24. Tzoof - de•vash eem•rei - no•am ma•tok la•ne•fesh oo•mar•pe la•a•tzem.

Temple Mount and the al-Aqsa Mosque, Jerusalem, Israel

*To everything there is a season, A time for every purpose under heaven: A time to be born, And a time to die; A time to plant, And a time to pluck what is planted; A time to kill, And a time to **heal**; A time to break down, And a time to build up.*

Ecclesiastes 3:1-3

א. לַכֹּל זְמָן וְעֵת לְכָל-חֵפֶץ תַּחַת הַשָּׁמָיִם:

ב. עֵת לָלֶדֶת וְעֵת לָמוּת עֵת לָטַעַת וְעֵת לַעֲקוֹר נָטוּעַ:

ג. עֵת לַהֲרוֹג וְעֵת לִרְפּוֹא עֵת לִפְרוֹץ וְעֵת לִבְנוֹת:

1. La•kol ze•man ve•et le•chol - che•fetz ta•chat ha•sha•ma•yim.
2. Et la•le•det ve•et la•moot et la•ta•at ve•et la•a•kor na•tooa.
3. Et la•ha•rog ve•et lir•po et lif•rotz ve•et liv•not.

Dome of the Rock and Temple Mount in Jerusalem, Israel

CONFESSING THE HEBREW SCRIPTURES

Adonai – Jehovah Rof•e•cha – יְהוָה רֹפְאֶךָ
"THE LORD YOUR HEALER"

*Moreover the light of the moon will be as the light of the sun, And the light of the sun will be sevenfold, As the light of seven days, In the day that the Lord binds up the bruise of His people And **heals** the stroke of their wound.*

Isaiah 30:26

וְהָיָה אוֹר-הַלְּבָנָה כְּאוֹר הַחַמָּה וְאוֹר הַחַמָּה יִהְיֶה
שִׁבְעָתַיִם כְּאוֹר שִׁבְעַת הַיָּמִים בְּיוֹם חֲבֹשׁ יְהוָה
אֶת-שֶׁבֶר עַמּוֹ וּמַחַץ מַכָּתוֹ יִרְפָּא:

26. Ve•ha•ya or - hal•va•na ke•or ha•cha•ma ve•or ha•cha•ma yi•hi•ye
shiv•ata•yim ke•or shiv•at ha•ya•mim be•yom cha•vosh Adonai
et - she•ver amo oo•ma•chatz ma•ka•to yir•pa.

Pool of Bethesda, Jerusalem, Israel

CONFESSING THE HEBREW SCRIPTURES

Adonai – Jehovah Rof•e•cha – יְהֹוָה רֹפְאֶךָ
"THE LORD YOUR HEALER"

*B*ut He was wounded for our transgressions, He was bruised for our iniquities; The chastisement for our peace was upon Him, And by His stripes we are **healed**.

Isaiah 53:5

וְהוּא מְחֹלָל מִפְּשָׁעֵנוּ מְדֻכָּא מֵעֲוֹנֹתֵינוּ מוּסַר שְׁלוֹמֵנוּ
עָלָיו וּבַחֲבֻרָתוֹ נִרְפָּא-לָנוּ׃

5. Ve•hoo me•cho•lal mip•sha•e•noo me•doo•ka me•avo•no•tei•noo moo•sar sh'lo•me•noo a•lav oo•va•cha•voo•ra•to nir•pa - la•noo.

Looking out over the harbor entrance at Jaffa

CONFESSING THE HEBREW SCRIPTURES

Adonai – Jehovah Rof•e•cha – יְהֹוָה רֹפְאֶךָ
"THE LORD YOUR HEALER"

*I have seen his ways, and will **heal** him; I will also lead him, And restore comforts to him And to his mourners.*

*"I create the fruit of the lips: Peace, peace to him who is far off and to him who is near," Says the Lord, "And I will **heal** him."*

Isaiah 57:18-19

דְּרָכָיו רָאִיתִי וְאֶרְפָּאֵהוּ וְאַנְחֵהוּ וַאֲשַׁלֵּם נִחֻמִים לוֹ וְלַאֲבֵלָיו:
בּוֹרֵא (נוב) [נִיב] שְׂפָתָיִם שָׁלוֹם שָׁלוֹם לָרָחוֹק וְלַקָּרוֹב
אָמַר יְהֹוָה וּרְפָאתִיו:

18. D'ra•chav ra•ee•ti ve•er•pa•e•hoo ve•an•che•hoo va•a•sha•lem ni•choo•mim lo ve•la•a•ve•lav.

19. Bo•re (niv) [niv] se•fa•ta•yim sha•lom sha•lom la•ra•chok ve•la•ka•rov amar Adonai oor•fa•tiv.

Ancient olive grove in the Galilee, Israel

CONFESSING THE HEBREW SCRIPTURES

Adonai – Jehovah Rof•e•cha – יְהֹוָה רֹפְאֶךָ
"THE LORD YOUR HEALER"

*T*hen your light shall break forth like the morning, Your **healing** shall spring forth speedily, And your righteousness shall go before you; The glory of the Lord shall be your rear guard.

Isaiah 58:8

אָז יִבָּקַע כַּשַּׁחַר אוֹרֶךָ וַאֲרֻכָתְךָ מְהֵרָה תִצְמָח וְהָלַךְ לְפָנֶיךָ צִדְקֶךָ כְּבוֹד יְהוָה יַאַסְפֶךָ:

8. Az yi•ba•ka ka•sha•char o•re•cha va•a•roo•chat•cha me•he•ra titz•mach ve•ha•lach le•fa•ne•cha tzid•ke•cha ke•vod Adonai ya•as•fe•cha.

Colonnade of the ruins of ancient temple in Ovdat, Israel

"*The Spirit of the Lord God is upon Me, Because the Lord has anointed Me To preach good tidings to the poor; He has sent Me to **heal** the brokenhearted, To proclaim liberty to the captives, And the opening of the prison to those who are bound;*

Isaiah 61:1

רוּחַ אֲדֹנָי יֱהוִה עָלָי יַעַן מָשַׁח יְהוָה אֹתִי לְבַשֵּׂר עֲנָוִים שְׁלָחַנִי לַחֲבֹשׁ לְנִשְׁבְּרֵי-לֵב לִקְרֹא לִשְׁבוּיִם דְּרוֹר וְלַאֲסוּרִים פְּקַח-קוֹחַ:

1. Roo•ach Adonai Elohim a•lai ya•an ma•shach Adonai o•ti le•va•ser ana•vim sh'la•cha•ni la•cha•vosh le•nish•be•rei - lev lik•ro lish•voo•yim de•ror ve•la•a•soo•rim pe•kach - ko•ach.

The multi-colored sandstone hills in the Sinai Desert, Israel

CONFESSING THE HEBREW SCRIPTURES

Adonai – Jehovah Rof•e•cha – יְהוָה רֹפְאֶךָ
"THE LORD YOUR HEALER"

"*Return, you backsliding children, And I will **heal** your backslidings.*" "*Indeed we do come to You, For You are the Lord our God.*

Jeremiah 3:22

שׁוּבוּ בָּנִים שׁוֹבָבִים אֶרְפָּה מְשׁוּבֹתֵיכֶם הִנְנוּ אָתָנוּ לָךְ כִּי אַתָּה יְהוָה אֱלֹהֵינוּ:

22. Shoo•voo ba•nim sho•va•vim er•pa me•shoo•vo•tei•chem hi•ne•noo ata•noo lach ki ata Adonai Elo•hey•noo.

Notes to God in the Western Wall in Jerusalem, Israel

*Heal me, O Lord, and I shall be **healed**; Save me, and I shall be saved, For You are my praise.*

Jeremiah 17:14

רְפָאֵנִי יְהוָה וְאֵרָפֵא הוֹשִׁיעֵנִי וְאִוָּשֵׁעָה כִּי תְהִלָּתִי אָתָּה:

14. Re•fa•eni Adonai ve•era•fe ho•shi•eni ve•ee•va•she•ah ki te•hi•la•ti ata.

Ruins of ancient fortress, Masada, Israel

CONFESSING THE HEBREW SCRIPTURES

Adonai – Jehovah Rof•e•cha – יְהוָה רֹפְאֶךָ
"THE LORD YOUR HEALER"

*'F*or I will restore **health** to you And **heal** you of your wounds,' says the Lord, 'Because they called you an outcast saying: "This is Zion; No one seeks her." '

Jeremiah 30:17

כִּי אַעֲלֶה אֲרֻכָה לָךְ וּמִמַּכּוֹתַיִךְ אֶרְפָּאֵךְ נְאֻם־יְהוָה כִּי נִדָּחָה קָרְאוּ לָךְ צִיּוֹן הִיא דֹּרֵשׁ אֵין לָהּ:

17. Ki aa•le aroo•cha lach oo•mi•ma•ko•ta•yich er•pa•ech n'oom - Adonai ki ni•da•cha kar•oo lach Tzi•yon hi do•resh eyn la.

Mountain and coastal line in the Dead Sea, Israel

CONFESSING THE HEBREW SCRIPTURES

Adonai – Jehovah Rof•e•cha – יְהוָֹה רֹפְאֶךָ

"THE LORD YOUR HEALER"

'*Behold, I will bring it* **health** *and* **healing**; *I will* **heal** *them and reveal to them the abundance of peace and truth.*'

Jeremiah 33:6

הִנְנִי מַעֲלֶה-לָּה אֲרֻכָה וּמַרְפֵּא וּרְפָאתִם וְגִלֵּיתִי לָהֶם
עֲתֶרֶת שָׁלוֹם וֶאֱמֶת:

6. Hi•ne•ni ma•a•le - la aroo•cha oo•mar•pe oor•fa•tim ve•gi•le•ti la•hem ate•ret sha•lom ve•emet.

View of the Dead Sea from the ancient city of Masada, Israel

CONFESSING THE HEBREW SCRIPTURES

Adonai – Jehovah Rof•e•cha – יְהֹוָה רֹפְאֶךָ
"THE LORD YOUR HEALER"

*Then he said to me: "This water flows toward the eastern region, goes down into the valley, and enters the sea. When it reaches the sea, its waters are **healed**.*

*"And it shall be that every living thing that moves, wherever the rivers go, will live. There will be a very great multitude of fish, because these waters go there; for they will be **healed**, and everything will live wherever the river goes."*   Ezekiel 47:8-9

וַיֹּאמֶר אֵלַי הַמַּיִם הָאֵלֶּה יֹצְאִים אֶל-הַגְּלִילָה הַקַּדְמוֹנָה
וְיָרְדוּ עַל-הָעֲרָבָה וּבָאוּ הַיָּמָה אֶל-הַיָּמָה הַמּוּצָאִים
(וְנִרְפָּאוּ) [וְנִרְפּוּ] הַמָּיִם:
וְהָיָה כָל-נֶפֶשׁ חַיָּה אֲשֶׁר-יִשְׁרֹץ אֶל כָּל-אֲשֶׁר יָבוֹא שָׁם
נַחֲלַיִם יִחְיֶה וְהָיָה הַדָּגָה רַבָּה מְאֹד כִּי בָאוּ שָׁמָּה הַמַּיִם
הָאֵלֶּה וְיֵרָפְאוּ וָחַי כֹּל אֲשֶׁר-יָבוֹא שָׁמָּה הַנָּחַל:

8. Va•yo•mer e•lai ha•ma•yim ha•e•le yotz•eem el - hag•li•la ha•kad•mo•na ve•yar•doo al - ha•Ara•va oo•va•oo ha•ya•ma el - ha•ya•ma ha•moo•tza•eem (ve•nir•poo) [ve•nir•poo] ha•ma•yim.

9. Ve•ha•ya chol - ne•fesh cha•ya asher - yish•rotz el kol - asher ya•vo sham na•cha•la•yim yich•ye ve•ha•ya ha•da•ga ra•ba me•od ki va•oo sha•ma ha•ma•yim ha•e•le ve•ye•raf•oo va•chai kol asher - ya•vo sha•ma ha•na•chal.

Holy Land mosaic, Israel

CONFESSING THE HEBREW SCRIPTURES

Adonai – Jehovah Rof•e•cha – יְהֹוָה רֹפְאֶךָ

"THE LORD YOUR HEALER"

*C*ome, and let us return to the Lord; For He has torn, but He will **heal** us; He has stricken, but He will bind us up.

Hosea 6:1

לְכוּ וְנָשׁוּבָה אֶל-יְהֹוָה כִּי הוּא טָרָף וְיִרְפָּאֵנוּ יַךְ וְיַחְבְּשֵׁנוּ:

1. Le•choo ve•na•shoo•va el - Adonai ki hoo ta•raf ve•yir•pa•e•noo yach ve•yach•be•she•noo.

Sea of Galilee in the early morning, Israel

CONFESSING THE HEBREW SCRIPTURES

Adonai – Jehovah Rof•e•cha – יְהֹוָה רֹפְאֶ֑ךָ

"THE LORD YOUR HEALER"

*But to you who fear My name The Sun of Righteousness shall arise With **healing** in His wings; And you shall go out And grow fat like stall-fed calves.*

Malachi 4:2

וְזָרְחָה לָכֶם יִרְאֵי שְׁמִי שֶׁמֶשׁ צְדָקָה וּמַרְפֵּא בִּכְנָפֶיהָ
וִיצָאתֶם וּפִשְׁתֶּם כְּעֶגְלֵי מַרְבֵּק:

20. Ve•zar•cha la•chem yir•ey sh'mi she•mesh tze•da•ka oo•mar•pe bich•na•fe•ha viy•tza•tem oo•fish•tem ke•eg•lei mar•bek.

NOTE: In the Hebrew Bible, it is 3:20.

Ruins of the great synagogue of Capernaum, Israel

*T*hen His fame went throughout all Syria; and they brought to Him all sick people who were afflicted with various diseases and torments, and those who were demon-possessed, epileptics, and paralytics; and He **healed** them.

Matthew 4:24

וַיֵּצֵא שָׁמְעוֹ בְּכָל-אֶרֶץ סוּרְיָא וַיָּבִיאוּ אֵלָיו אֵת כָּל-הַחוֹלִים אֲשֶׁר דָּבְקוּ בָם תַּחֲלָאִים שׁוֹנִים וְחָלָיִם רָעִים אֲחֻזֵי רוּחוֹת רָעוֹת מֻכֵּי יָרֵחַ וּנְכֵי עֲצָמוֹת וַיִּרְפָּאֵם:

24. Va•ye•tze shim•oh be•chol - eretz Soor•ya va•ya•vi•oo elav et kol - ha•cho•lim asher dav•koo vam ta•cha•loo•eem sho•nim va•cho•la•yim ra•eem achoo•zey roo•chot ra•ot moo•key ya•re•ach oon•chey a•tza•mot va•yir•pa•em.

Jordan River, Israel

CONFESSING THE HEBREW SCRIPTURES

Adonai – Jehovah Rof•e•cha – יְהֹוָה רֹפְאֶךָ

"THE LORD YOUR HEALER"

*The centurion answered and said, "Lord, I am not worthy that You should come under my roof. But only speak a word, and my servant will be **healed**."*

Matthew 8:8

וַיַּעַן שַׂר-הַמֵּאָה וַיֹּאמַר אֲדֹנִי נְקַלֹּתִי מִזֹּאת כִּי אַתָּה תָבֹא
בְּצֵל קֹרָתִי אַךְ רַק דַּבְּרָה דָבָר וְהַנַּעַר יֶחִי:

8. Va•ya•an sar - ha•me•ah va•yo•mar Adoni n`ka•lo•ti mi•zot ki ata ta•vo ve•tzel ko•ra•ti ach rak dab•ra da•var ve•ha•na•ar ye•chi.

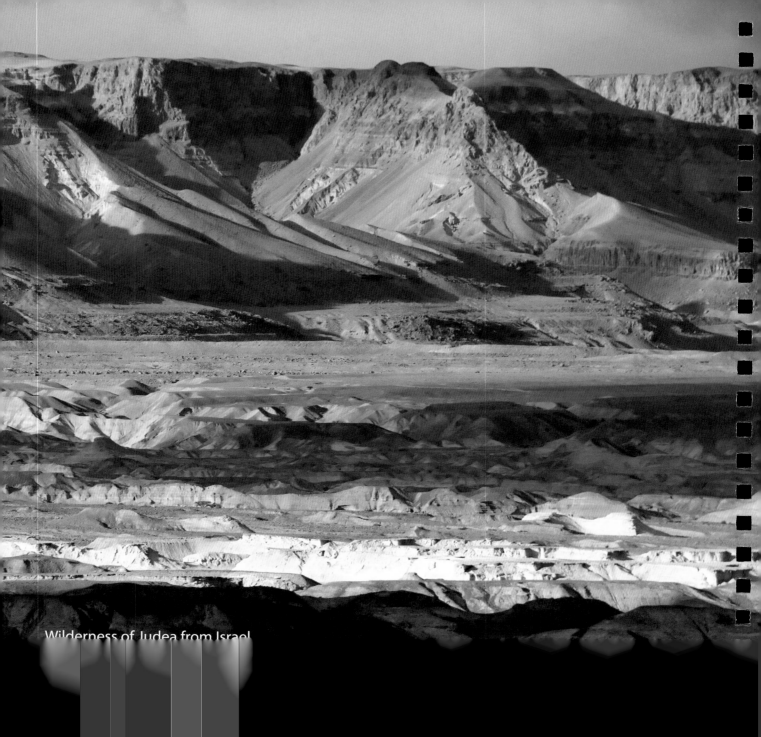

Wilderness of Judea from Israel

*T*hen Jesus said to the centurion, *"Go your way; and as you have believed, so let it be done for you." And his servant was* **healed** *that same hour.*

Matthew 8:13

וְאֶל-שַׂר-הַמֵּאָה אָמַר יֵשׁוּעַ לֵךְ כַּאֲשֶׁר הֶאֱמַנְתָּ כֵּן יָקוּם

לָךְ וַיְחִי הַנַּעַר מֵחָלְיוֹ בַּשָּׁעָה הַהִיא:

13. Ve•el - sar - ha•me•ah amar Yeshua lech ka•a•sher he•e•man•ta ken ya•koom lach vay•chi ha•na•ar me•chol•yo ba•sha•ah ha•hee.

Falls and the river in reserve on the Dead Sea, Israel

*When evening had come, they brought to Him many who were demon-possessed. And He cast out the spirits with a word, and **healed** all who were sick...*

Matthew 8:16

וַיְהִי בָעֶרֶב וַיָּבִיאוּ אֵלָיו רַבִּים אֲשֶׁר דָּבְקוּ בָּם רוּחוֹת רָעוֹת
וַיְגָרֶשׁ אֶת-הָרוּחוֹת בִּדְבַר-פִּיו וְאֵת כָּל-הַחוֹלִים הֶחֱיָה מֵחָלְיָם:

16. Vay•hi ba•e•rev va•ya•vi•oo elav ra•bim asher dav•koo bam roo•chot ra•ot va•y`ga•resh et - ha•roo•chot bid•var - piv ve•et kol - ha•cho•lim he•che•ya me•chol•yam.

Mount Sinai in early morning light, Sinai Peninsula, Egypt

CONFESSING THE HEBREW SCRIPTURES

Adonai – Jehovah Rof•e•cha – יְהֹוָה רֹפְאֶךָ
"THE LORD YOUR HEALER"

*But when Jesus knew it, He withdrew from there; and great multitudes followed Him, and He **healed** them all.*

Matthew 12:15

וַיֵּדַע יֵשׁוּעַ וַיִּפֶן וַיֵּלֶךְ מִשָּׁם וַיֵּלֶךְ אַחֲרָיו הֲמוֹן עַם רָב
וַיְרַפֵּא אֶת-כֻּלָם:

15. Va•ye•da Yeshua va•yi•fen va•ye•lech mi•sham va•ye•lech a•cha•rav ha•mon am rav vay•ra•pe et - koo•lam.

Ruins of the ancient synagogue at Capernaum, Israel

Adonai – Jehovah Rof•e•cha – יְהוָֹה רֹפְאֶךָ
"THE LORD YOUR HEALER"

*Then one was brought to Him who was demon-possessed, blind and mute; and He **healed** him, so that the blind and mute man both spoke and saw.*

Matthew 12:22

אָז הוּבָא לְפָנָיו אִישׁ עִוֵּר וְאִלֵּם אֲשֶׁר רוּחַ רָע דָּבַק בּוֹ
וַיִּרְפָּאֵהוּ וְהָעִוֵּר הָאִלֵּם דִּבֶּר וְרָאָה:

22. Az hoo•va le•fa•nav eesh ee•ver ve•ee•lem asher roo•ach ra da•vak bo va•yir•pa•e•hoo ve•ha•ee•ver ha•ee•lem di•ber ve•ra•ah.

Negev Valley, Israel

CONFESSING THE HEBREW SCRIPTURES

Adonai – Jehovah Rof•e•cha – יְהֹוָה רֹפְאֶךָ
"THE LORD YOUR HEALER"

*A*nd when Jesus went out He saw a great multitude; and He was moved with compassion for them, and **healed** their sick.

Matthew 14:14

וַיֵּצֵא יֵשׁוּעַ וַיַּרְא הֲמוֹן עַם-רָב וְרַחֲמָיו נִכְמְרוּ עֲלֵיהֶם וַיִּרְפָּא אֶת-חוֹלֵיהֶם:

14. Va•ye•tze Yeshua va•yar ha•mon am - rav ve•ra•cha•mav nich•me•roo aley•hem va•yir•pa et - cho•ley•hem.

Tower of David, Western Wall, Jerusalem, Israel

*Then Jesus answered and said to her, "O woman, great is your faith! Let it be to you as you desire." And her daughter was **healed** from that very hour.*

Matthew 15:28

וַיַּעַן יֵשׁוּעַ וַיֹּאמֶר אֵלֶיהָ אִשָּׁה גְדוֹלָה אֱמוּנָתֵךְ יְהִי-לָךְ כַּאֲשֶׁר עִם-לְבָבֵךְ וַתֵּרָפֵא בִתָּהּ בָּעֵת הַהִיא:

28. Va•ya•an Yeshua va•yo•mer e•le•ha ee•sha ge•do•la emoo•na•tech ye•hee - lach ka•a•sher eem - le•va•vech va•te•ra•fe vi•ta ba•et ha•hee.

Arch of Titus, Jerusalem, Israel

CONFESSING THE HEBREW SCRIPTURES

Adonai – Jehovah Rof•e•cha – יְהוָה רֹפְאֶךָ

"THE LORD YOUR HEALER"

*Then great multitudes came to Him, having with them the lame, blind, mute, maimed, and many others; and they laid them down at Jesus' feet, and He **healed** them.*

Matthew 15:30

וַיָּבֹאוּ לְפָנָיו הֲמוֹן עַם-רָב וְעִמָּהֶם פִּסְחִים עִוְרִים חֵרְשִׁים נִדְכָּאִים וְרַבִּים כְּמוֹהֶם וַיַּצִּיגוּם לְרַגְלֵי יֵשׁוּעַ וְהוּא רִפָּא אֹתָם:

30. Va•ya•vo•oo le•fa•nav ha•mon am - rav ve•ee•ma•hem pis•chim eev•rim cher•shim nid•ka•eem ve•ra•bim ke•mo•hem va•ya•tzi•goom le•rag•ley Yeshua ve•hoo ri•pa o•tam.

Wailing Wall, Jerusalem, Israel

CONFESSING THE HEBREW SCRIPTURES

Adonai – Jehovah Rof•e•cha – יְהוָה רֹפְאֶךָ
"THE LORD YOUR HEALER"

*A*nd great multitudes followed Him, and He **healed** them there.

Matthew 19:2

וַהֲמוֹן עַם־רָב הָלְכוּ אַחֲרָיו וַיִּרְפָּאֵם שָׁם מֵחָלְיָם:

2. Va•ha•mon am - rav hal•choo a•cha•rav va•yir•pa•em sham me•chol•yam.

Shepherd and his flock, Israel

CONFESSING THE HEBREW SCRIPTURES

Adonai – Jehovah Rof•e•cha – יְהֹוָה רֹפְאֶךָ
"THE LORD YOUR HEALER"

*Then the blind and the lame came to Him in the temple, and He **healed** them.*

Matthew 21:14

וַיִּגְּשׁוּ אֵלָיו עִוְרִים וּפִסְחִים בְּבֵית הַמִּקְדָּשׁ וַיִּרְפָּאֵם:

14. Va•yig•shoo elav eev•rim oo•fis•chim be•veit ha•mik•dash va•yir•pa•em.

Landscape of Judea Mountains near Dead Sea

*Now as the lame man who was **healed** held on to Peter and John, all the people ran together to them in the porch which is called Solomon's, greatly amazed.*

Acts 3:11

וְהוּא כִּי דָבַק אַחֲרֵי פֶּטְרוֹס וְיוֹחָנָן וְכָל-הָעָם רָצוּ אֲלֵיהֶם אֶל-הָאוּלָם הַנִּקְרָא אוּלָם שְׁלֹמֹה וַיִּשְׁמוּ עַד-מְאֹד:

11. Ve•hoo chi da•vak a•cha•rey Fetros ve•Yo•cha•nan ve•chol - ha•am ra•tzoo aley•hem el - ha•oo•lam ha•nik•ra Oo•lam Sh`lo•mo va•ya•sho•moo ad - me•od.

View from Mount Carmel, Western Galilee, Israel

CONFESSING THE HEBREW SCRIPTURES

Adonai – Jehovah Rof•e•cha – יְהֹוָה רֹפְאֶךָ

"THE LORD YOUR HEALER"

*And seeing the man who had been **healed** standing with them, they could say nothing against it.*

Acts 4:14

וּבִרְאֹתָם אֶת-הָאִישׁ הַנִּרְפָּא עֹמֵד עִמָּהֶם לֹא יָכְלוּ לַעֲנוֹת בָּם דָּבָר:

14. Oo•vir•o•tam et - ha•eesh ha•nir•pa o•med ee•ma•hem lo yach•loo la•a•not bam da•var.

Tower of David, Jerusalem, Israel

CONFESSING THE HEBREW SCRIPTURES

Adonai – Jehovah Rof•e•cha – יְהֹוָה רֹפְאֶךָ

"THE LORD YOUR HEALER"

*A*lso a multitude gathered from the surrounding cities to
Jerusalem, bringing sick people and those who were tormented
by unclean spirits, and they were all **healed**.

Acts 5:16

וְגַם-הֲמוֹן עַם מִן-הֶעָרִים אֲשֶׁר מִסָּבִיב לִירוּשָׁלַיִם נָהֲרוּ
וַיָּבִיאוּ אֶת-הַחוֹלִים וְאֶת-הַנֶּעֱנִים תַּחַת יְדֵי רוּחוֹת טְמֵאוֹת
וְכֻלָּם נִרְפָּאוּ:

16. Ve•gam - ha•mon am min - he•a•rim asher mi•sa•viv
li•Ye•roo•sha•la•yim na•ha•roo va•ya•vi•oo et - ha•cho•lim ve•et -
ha•na•a•nim ta•chat ye•dey roo•chot t`me•ot ve•choo•lam nir•pa•oo.

Red hills by the Dead Sea, Israel

*Confess your trespasses to one another, and pray for one another, that you may be **healed**. The effective, fervent prayer of a righteous man avails much.*

James 5:16

לָכֵן הִתְוַדּוּ עֲוֹנוֹתֵיכֶם אִישׁ אֶל־רֵעֵהוּ וְהִתְפַּלְלוּ אִישׁ בְּעַד רֵעֵהוּ וְרָפָא לָכֶם כִּי־תְפִלַּת צַדִּיק רַב כֹּחַ בִּפְעֻלָּתָהּ:

16. La•chen hit•va•doo ao•no•tey•chem eesh el - re•e•hoo ve•hit•pa•le•loo eesh be•ad re•e•hoo ve•ra•fa la•chem ki - tefi•lat tza•dik rav ko•cha bif•oo•la•ta.

Jerusalem skyline, Israel

*W*ho Himself bore our sins in His own body on the tree, that we, having died to sins, might live for righteousness—by whose stripes you were **healed**.

1 Peter 2:24

וְהוּא נָשָׂא אֶת-חַטֹּאתֵינוּ בִּבְשָׂרוֹ עַל-הָעֵץ לְבַעֲבוּר נָמוּת
לַחֵטְאָ וְנִחְיֶה לִצְדָקָה וַאֲשֶׁר בַּחֲבֻרָתוֹ נִרְפָּא לָכֶם:

24. Ve•hoo na•sa et - cha•to•tey•noo biv•sa•ro al - ha•etz le•va•a•voor na•moot la•cha•ta•ah ve•nich•ye litz•da•ka va•a•sher ba•cha•voo•ra•to nir•pa la•chem.